The Mystery Cats of York

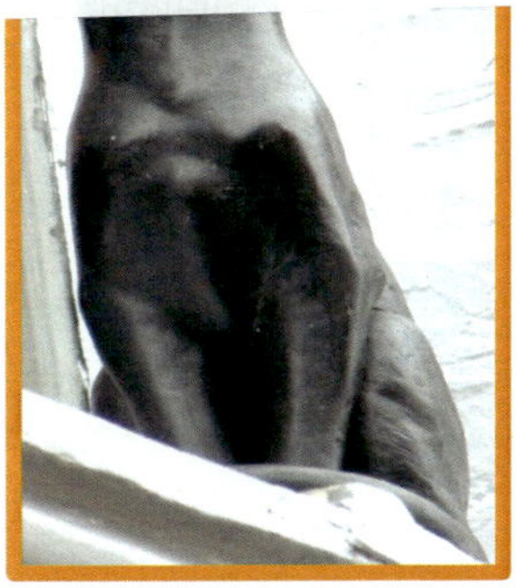

Where are they?
Who put them there?
Why are they there?
Who made them?

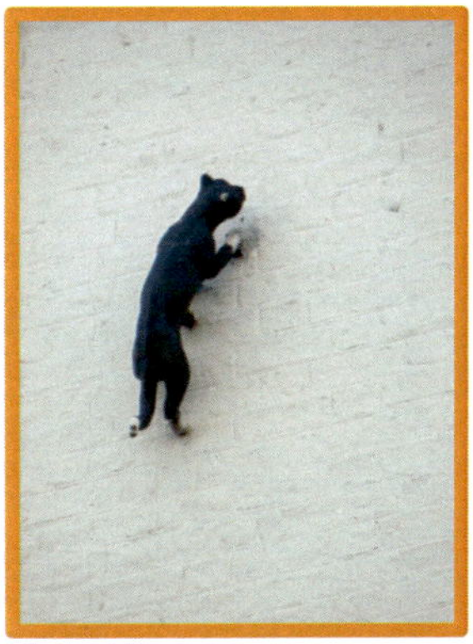

This book will help to answer these questions and guide you to the cats.

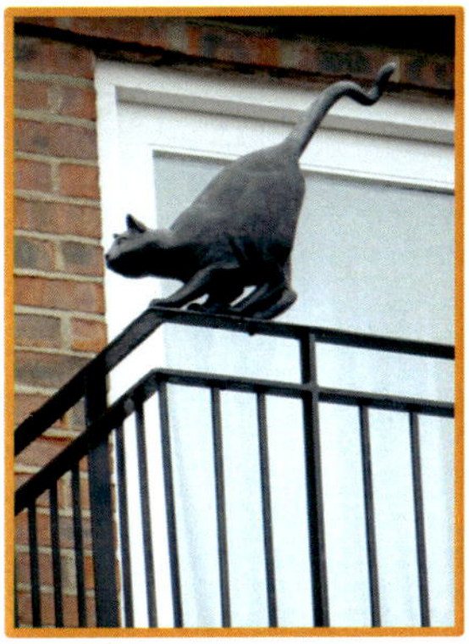

Stan Young
Jonathan Newdick
Brook Adams

Index Page

The Cat Letter relates to the location of the lettered cat on the map inside the front cover of this booklet and at the top of each photograph.

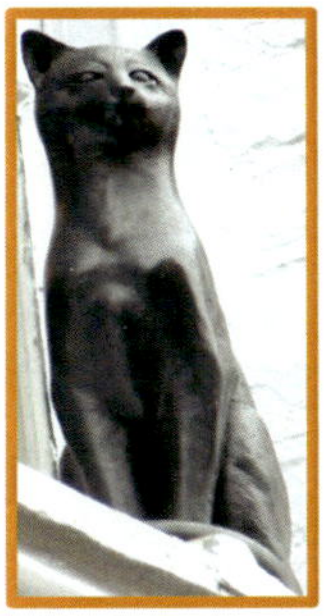

Welcome to the Mystery of the York Cats

York's interesting and varied streets and buildings can be even more engaging if one looks up rather than straight ahead. That's where you will find the cats!

In this book we will introduce you to 18 cats and show you where they are. Each page shows a close up of the cat and a view of the building or location where it 'resides'. You will need to examine some of the location or building photographs very closely to find the cat, some keep a low profile! Where it is known we will give you some history and context as to why the cat is in that particular location. Additionally, we will introduce you to the Architect, Tom Adams, whose idea it was to place the cats, and to Jonathan Newdick, the Sculptor, who made many of the cats. Each cat is identified by a name and a letter which you will find in the index and at the top of each cat photograph. The letter of each cat is used to identify it on the map inside the front cover.

Some of these pictures first appeared in a small exhibition at a retirement community in York and then at York Hospital. These exhibitions, and the positive reaction to them, created the impetus for this book. Many people commented that, even though they had lived in York for many years, or had visited many times, they had either been unaware of the cats as they seldom looked upward, or had seen a few of them but knew nothing about them. Others, familiar with the cats, expressed excitement that at last these hidden gems were getting the attention they deserved. As a result many undertook one of the Cat Trails!

In the process of assembling the exhibitions and this book I have benefitted enormously from the help of Jonathan Newdick and Brook Adams. Jonathan is the Sculptor commissioned by Tom, to make the cats, and Brook is Tom's son. They both generously shared their memories and information. I am indebted to them for their time and interest in this project and their full participation in the preparation of this publication. You can read more about both Tom and Jonathan on pages 25 to 29 in this book.

We hope you will enjoy this trail of discovery around York.

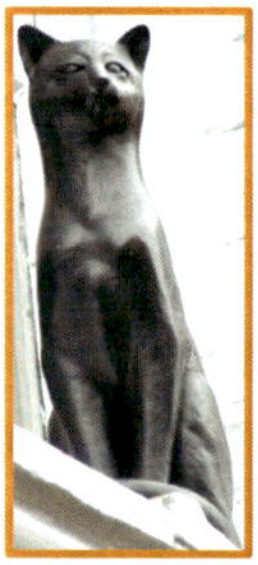

The Cats of York: an introduction...

For centuries cats have intrigued us. From the middle ages to the present day cats have been glorified or ridiculed. Whether being characterised as sacred symbols, as in Egypt, or as the essence of companionship, by individuals such as Patrick Moore or Ernest Hemingway, their combination of mystery, independence and cunning has fascinated us. Hence my interest in the silent and static cat sculptures of York and why I decided to find out more about them.

There are about 22 cat sculptures peering at us from window sills, door arches, walls and rooftops as we cross the city of York going about our business.

Together they make an unexpected and enjoyable find and form a 'trail' across the city and its fringes which can create an intriguing and amusing activity for adults and children alike. Cities, even beautiful York, can be busy, noisy and anonymous places so anything, which adds character, curiosity, a point of interest, or humour, seems to be important. I think the cats do all four things!

In this way Tom Adams, the Architect who initiated the idea, and Jonathan Newdick, the Sculptor who made many of the cats, have each made a unique contribution to York, one which is not found elsewhere, and one which continues to give ongoing pleasure to visitors and residents. Each cat has entailed a considerable amount of thought and planning. Sometimes planning consent was needed. The secure mounting of the cats was often complicated and involved many risky antics up ladders, hanging out of windows and even being hoisted up in cherry pickers! One or two of the photographs show the mounting of the cats but Jonathan Newdick has many tales to tell!

In keeping with their reputation as loners and survivors the cats prowl rooftops, cling to walls or simply sit and stare at the crowds and traffic below from windowsills and ledges. Folklore tells us that cats have been doing this in York for centuries. Originally, we understand, the belief was that this would frighten rats and mice away but we know that many recent cats have been placed simply to keep the tradition going and draw attention to a building. The earliest cats we are aware of are the two in Low Ousegate near Ouse Bridge (see page 15) which were reportedly placed there in the 1920's by the grocer who owned the shop and wished to frighten the vermin away! As for all the other cats…read on to find out!

The information about each cat has been gleaned from a variety of sources. The 'Cats in York' website and the 'Cat Trail Tour' leaflets produced by The Cat Gallery in Low Petergate and York Glass Ltd in The Shambles were useful starting points. Staff, or owners, in some of the shops and locations willingly shared anecdotes and memories where these were known.

However, it has to be said that given the passage of time, the accuracy of some of the information about each cat is difficult to verify or simply not known, particularly for those cats that did not originate from the work of Tom or Jonathan. This has not spoilt my enjoyment of discovering each cat and seeking out the history of the idea and I hope you will feel the same. Some local businesses have continued to commission cats so the tradition lives on and is still unique to York.

It is to be hoped that the cats we see today will continue to be looked after by their current and future owners and that they will live on as part of the varied landscape of the city.

I hope these photographs and cat tales will inspire you to look out for them...or even commission one for yourself!

This book will help you find and enjoy the cats. They are unique to York. I think this is the first publication that has brought many of them together along with information about their originators and history. It is a celebration not only of the work of Tom Adams, who believed that 'there should be fun in architecture' and Jonathan Newdick, but of the tradition which is still thriving.

Cat A: The Vegetarian Cat
Location: Goodramgate

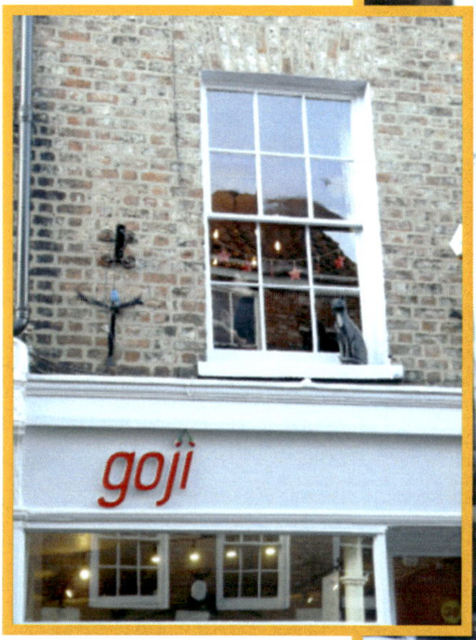

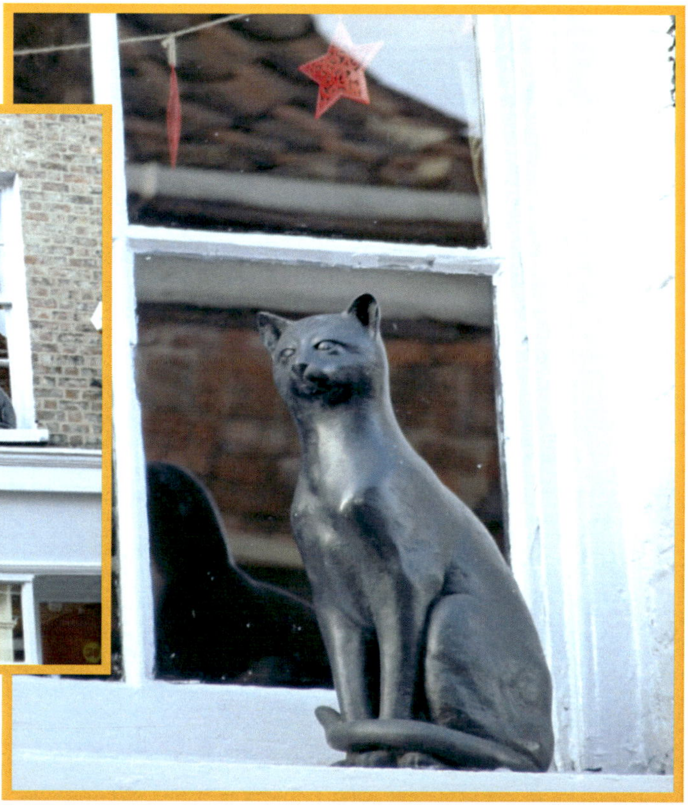

This black cat follows in the tradition of most black cats; apparently contented, proud and independent, composed, but watchful.

Positioned on his ledge in Goodramgate, he is the only cat in this part of town. He stares down towards The Shambles where his brother is climbing up the front of the York Glass shop (see page 24) next door to the historic shrine of Margaret Clitheroe. Both these cats were commissioned at the same time by York businessman John Hopkinson.

He is made of black resin but lacks the luminous eyes of some other cats in York.

Today he guards a vegetarian Cafe and Deli.

CAT B: Is the Cat stalking the Pigeon?
Location: Kings Square

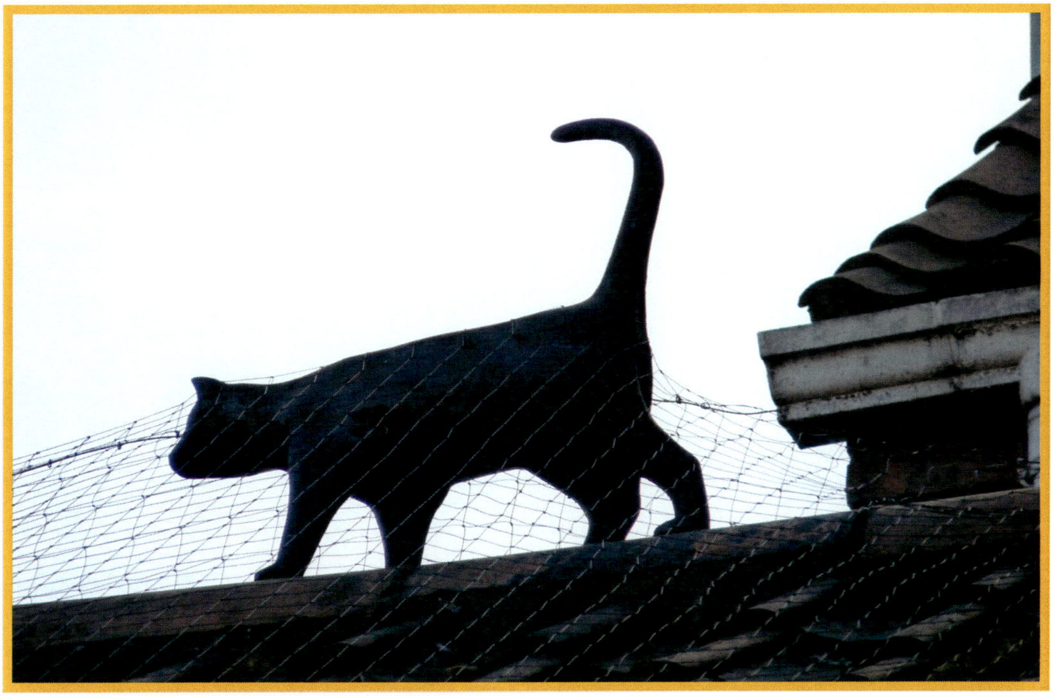

This is a Tom Adams Cat, made of black resin by the York Sculptor Jonathan Newdick.

The cat appeared during extension work in November 1984 on the building which overlooks Kings Square.

After the cat was installed it is alleged that the building's owner got a plumber, who was working on the property, to add a pigeon to the rooftop...(see photo. on the right) so it would now appear that the cat might be stalking the pigeon!

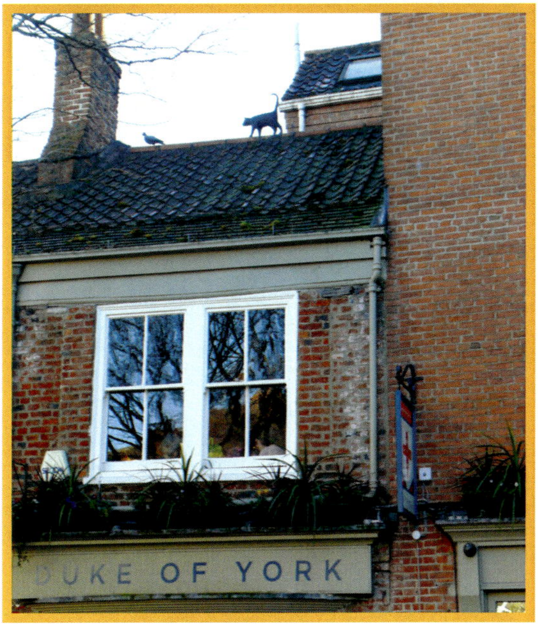

Cat C: Barnitts and their two cats
Location: Colliergate

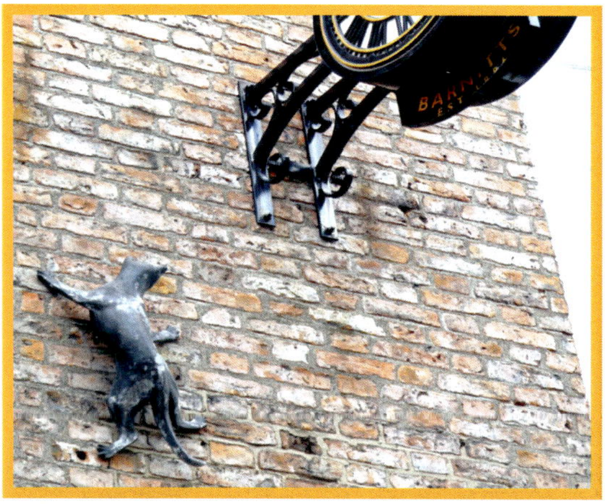

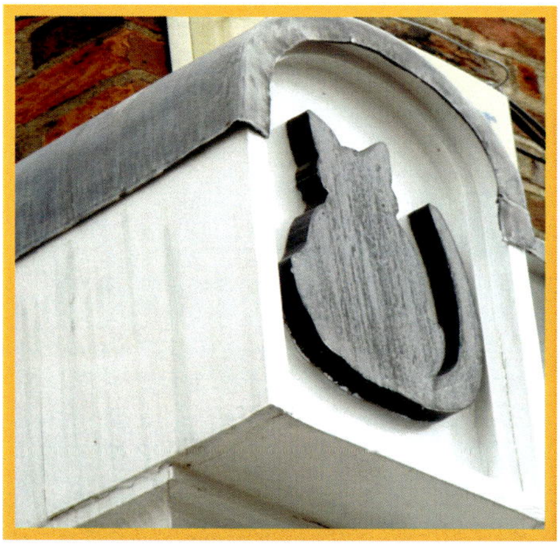

A Tom Adams cat!.

This cat, clinging to the brick wall under the clock at Barnitts, was made by Jonathan Newdick and placed after Tom died. The 'Cats in York' website reports that it was due to make its appearance in 2005 but alleged problems with planning permission delayed things. The owner of 'Barnitts' told the website that the cat (and the clock) was installed to celebrate her fathers' 50 years of service with the company.

Another Tom Adams cat!

This one isn't a statue. It is a silhouette and sits in a panel over one of the entrances to the shop.

The owners of Barnitts so loved the cats that they allowed Tom, who had worked on major renovations to their shop, to place a second one.

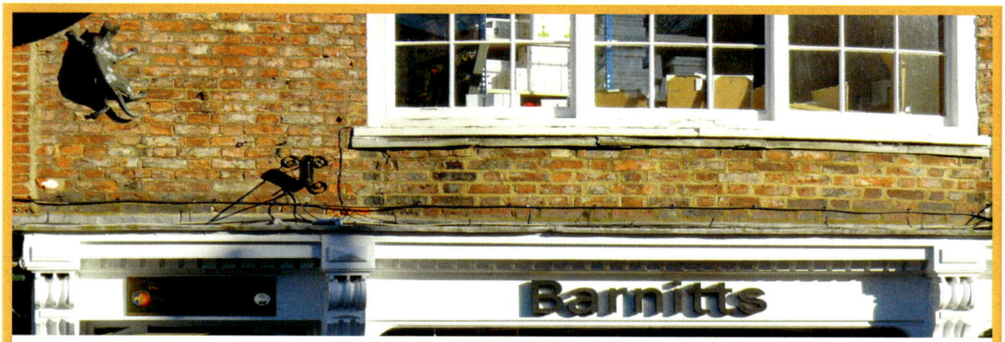

Cat D: The only kitten in the book
Location: St. Andrewgate

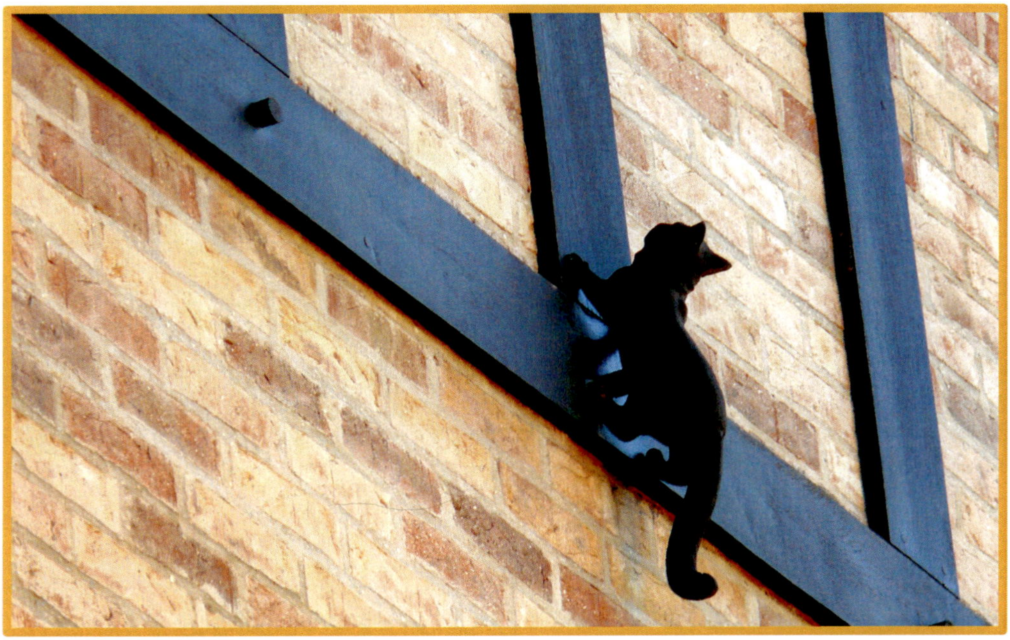

This is a kitten...not a cat, the only kitten in our collection in fact. It is a very brave kitten, very high up, and easily missed by pedestrians walking below. Can you spot him, or her, in the photograph opposite?

Although Tom Adams inspired, it is not a Jonathan Newdick sculpture but was, instead, purchased by Tom Adams from the nearby Garden Centre Department of Barnitts and sprayed black.

Perhaps it is being chased by the cat in the next page...just next door in St. Andrewgate? Or, it may have been trying to find its way home as Tom Adams lived near here!

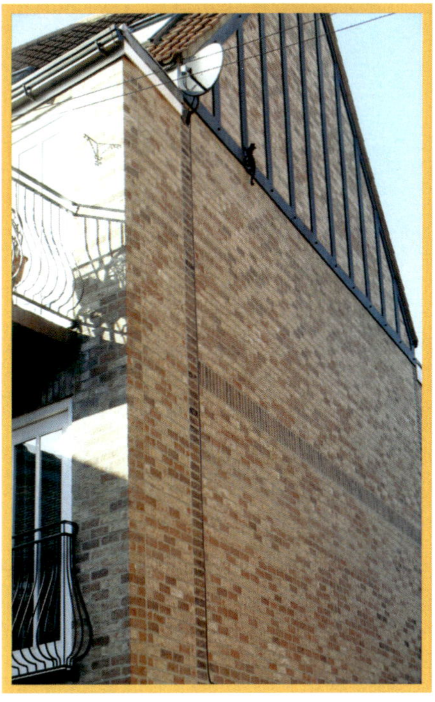

Cat E: The Balcony Cat....ready to pounce
Location: St Andrewgate

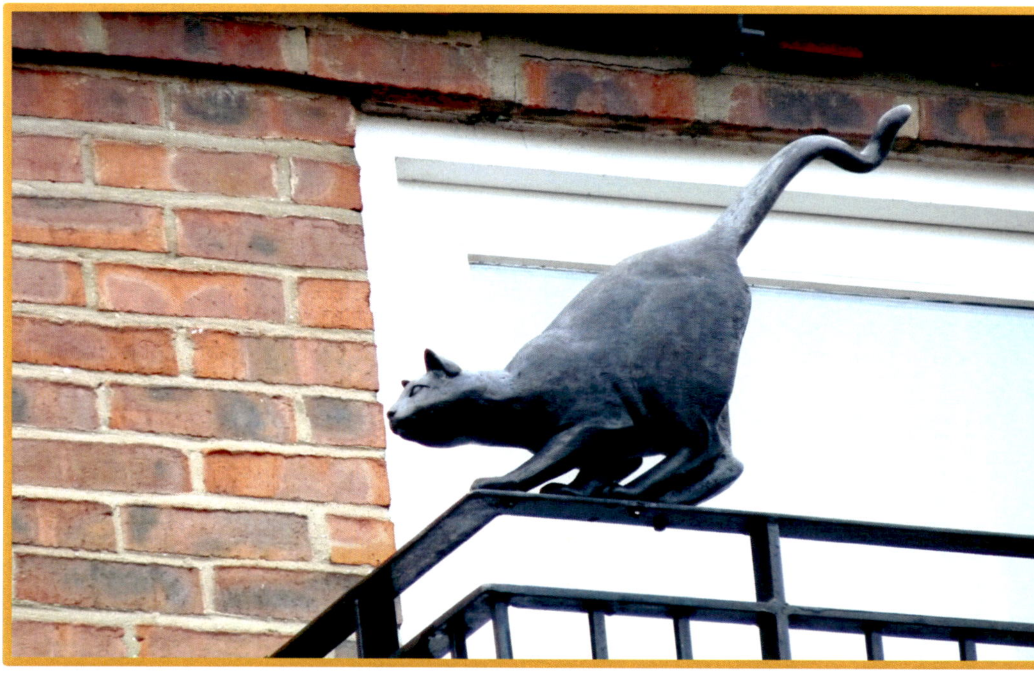

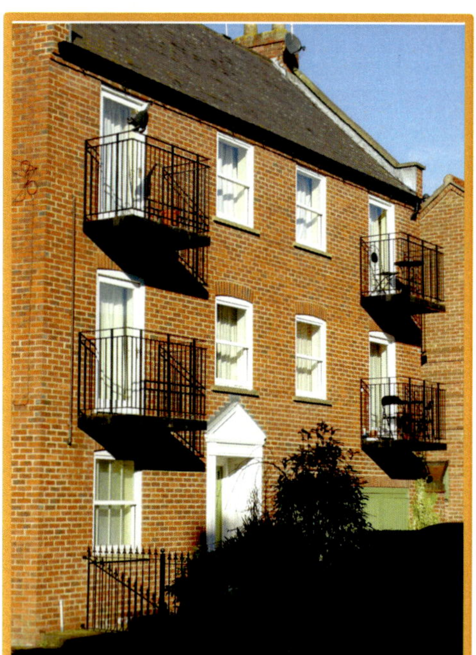

A Tom Adams inspired cat made by Jonathan Newdick. This cat usually prowls around a residential development in central York but this pose catches him, or her, as being agile, brave and ready to pounce.

This is one of the later cats, installed between 1999 and 2003. It is also one of the cats which was exhibited in the York Open Studios Exhibition in 2008 by Jonathan Newdick. It differs from many of the other more docile cats by showing itself ready for action.

I wonder if it is chasing the kitten on the building next door. See the previous page.

Cat F: The Climbing Cat on the Black Swan
Location : Peasholme Green

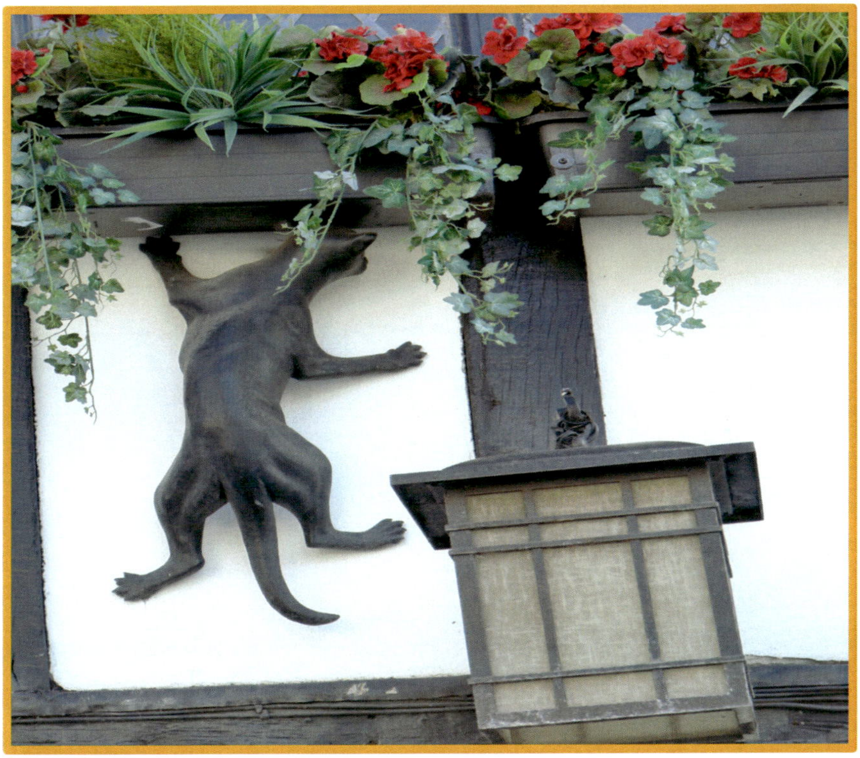

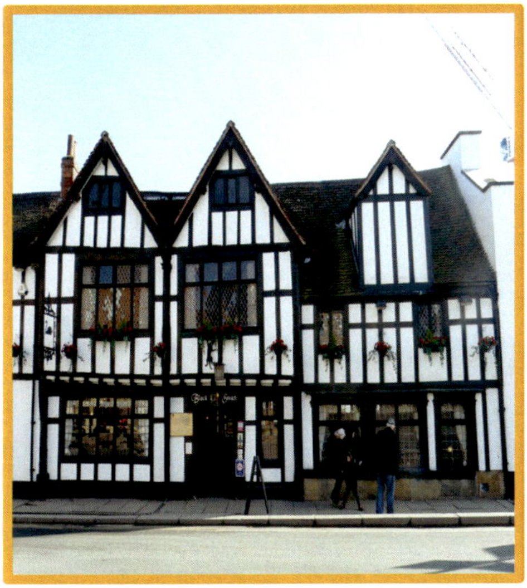

This very active cat is another of Jonathan Newdick's sculptures, placed here in 2010. It is modelled on Tom Adams's own cat, 'Mickey' (see page 25). It is climbing the wall above the doorway to one of the oldest pubs in York, The Black Swan in Peasholme Green.
Perhaps he or she is trying to escape from one of the many characters still thought to haunt the building. This building originated in the 15th century and was originally a house and is even built on the site of an earlier inn.

Cat G: The Ghostly Cat
Location: Pavement

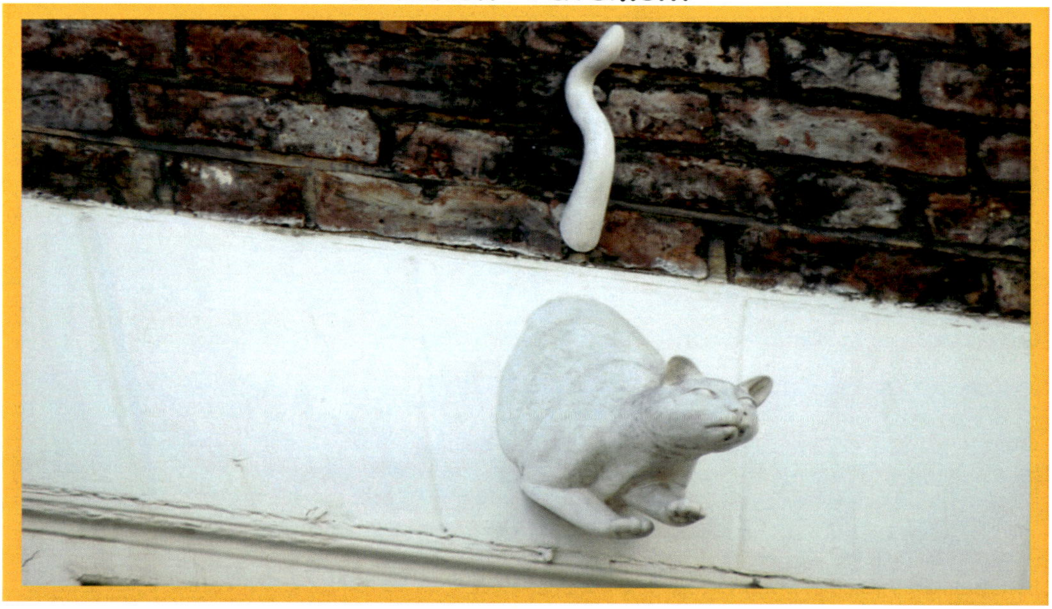

The Ghost Cat of York, another Jonathan Newdick cat placed here in 2011.
This cat, a shadow of it's former self, is seen emerging from above the first floor window on the front wall of this well known haunted pub in the centre of York. 'The Golden Fleece' has been an inn since 1667 and is one of the oldest pubs in the City. It's name refers to the importance of the woollen trade in York at that time.

'The Golden Fleece' is regarded as York's most haunted pub. It's walls are hung with photographs, reports of ghostly happenings and ghostly images. Lady Peckett, the wife of the pub's owner around 1700 is thought to be the resident ghost, reportedly seen by guests on many occasions!
Perhaps our cat has seen something, hence its ashen colour and frenzied escape route through the front wall of the building!

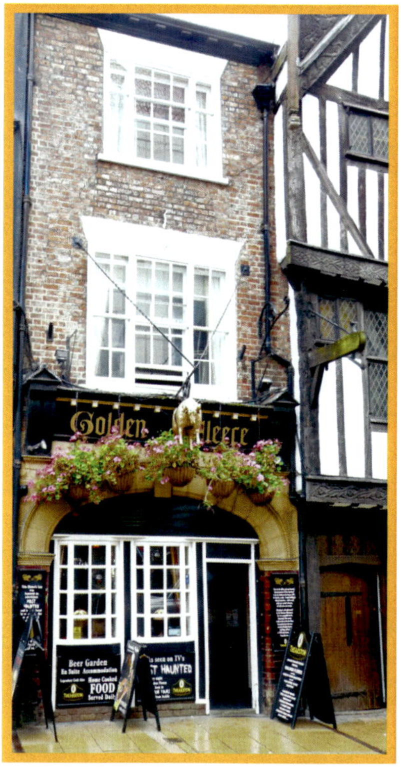

Cat H: The Cat who Guards the Ale
Location: Walmgate

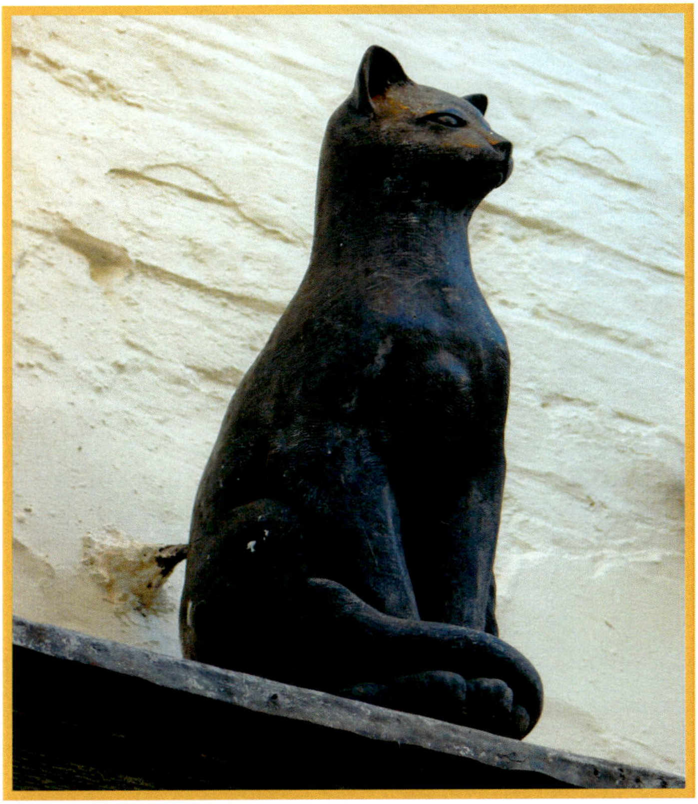

This upright and observant cat with its beautifully curled tail sits in Walmgate above what used to be 'MeltonsTwo' Cafe but is now an Ale House. It is a Tom Adams cat, made by Jonathan Newdick. The photograph below shows Tom Adams (Architect, left) with Jonathan Newdick (Sculptor, right) undertaking the difficult task of placing and securing the cat on this narrow ledge. This photo appeared in the York Press on 13.10.01.

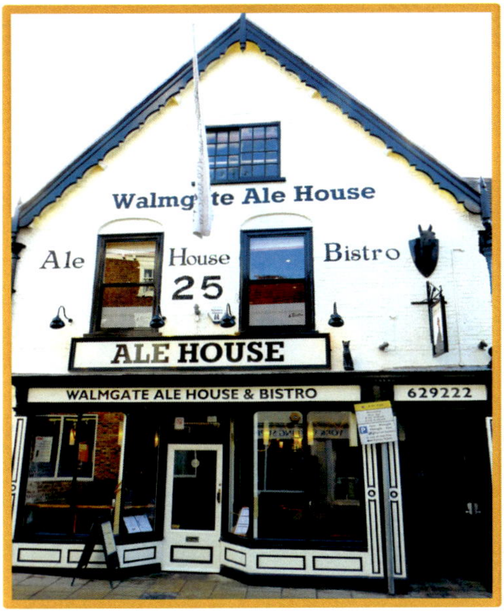

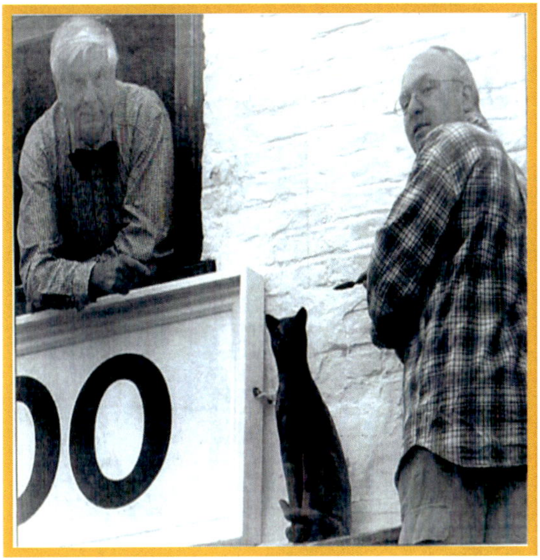

Cat I: The Oldest cats in the book

Location: Low Ousegate

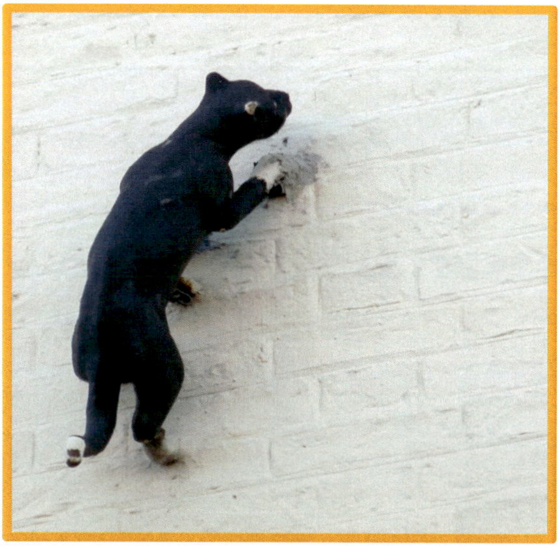

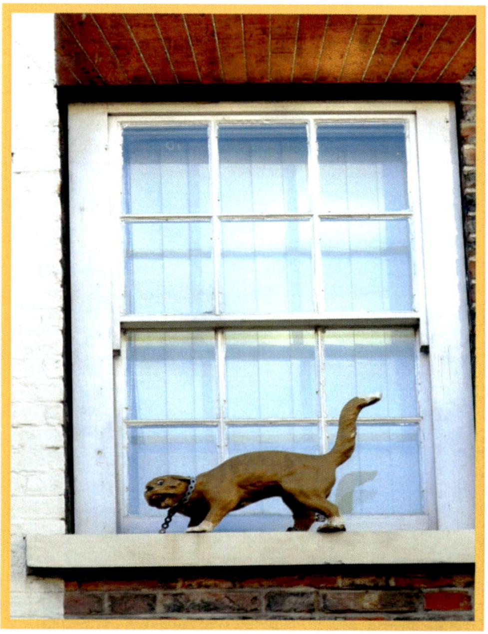

These two are thought to be the earliest cats still in place, probably dating from the 1920's, and live next door to each other in a prominent position near Ouse Bridge. The Evening Press (April 1962) says that Sir Stephen Aitcheson placed them there. He owned the grocer's business that occupied the building at that time.

They may have been put there to simply be an eye catching amusement, or, could they have been placed there in keeping with the folklore to scare the pigeons or mice?

Despite the ginger cat apparently being tethered, both cats have been stolen at different times over the years but like cats often do seem to have found their way back home!

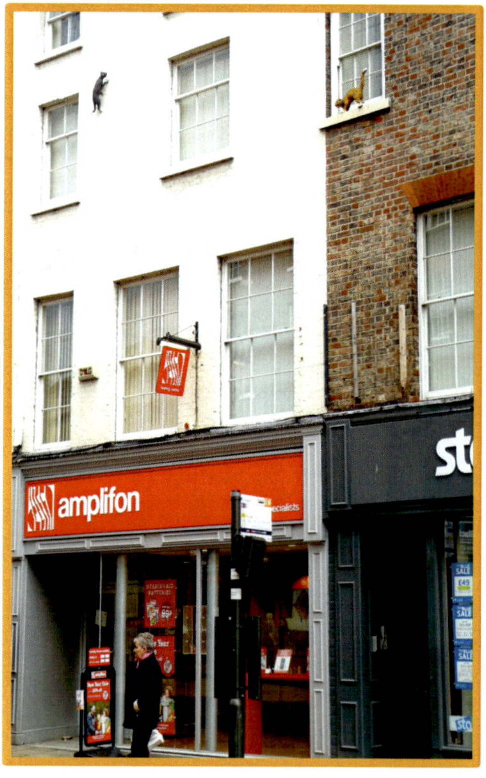

Cat J: The Lonely Prowler on the roof
Location: Overlooking the River Ouse, near Ouse Bridge

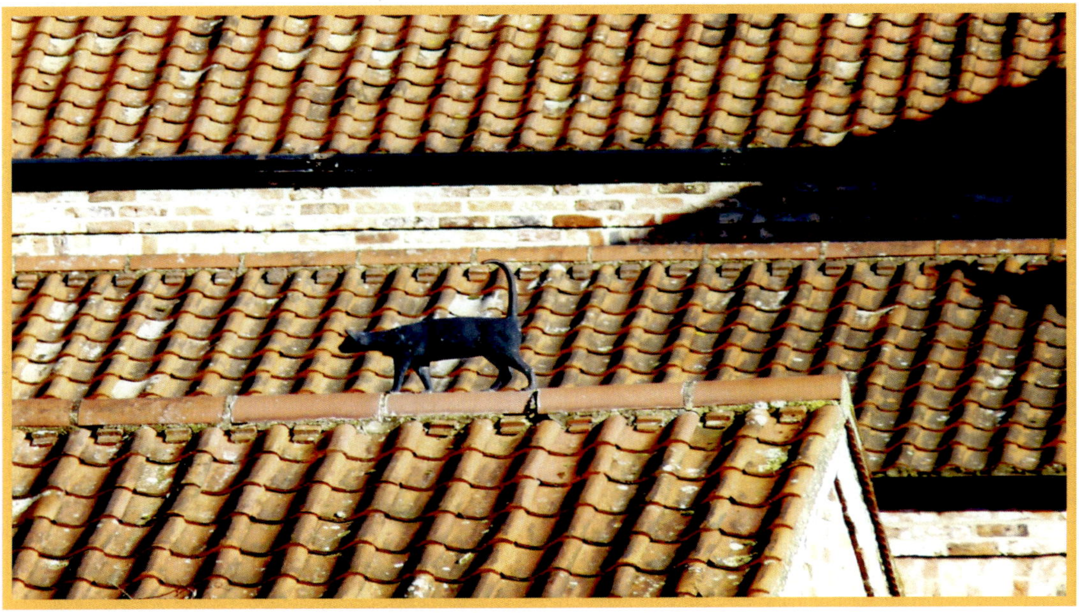

This roof prowler is the companion to the cat sitting on the windowsill of 25 Coney Street (see the next page). This is the rear of that building, seen only from the river.

It is one of Tom Adams' earliest cats, made by Jonathan Newdick. It featured in the York Press in April 1982.

The view above is seen from the riverwalk along the side of Piccolino's restaurant and the Park Inn. The view beside this panel is taken from the bridge (can you spot him?) and shows what a brave and lonesome cat this is!

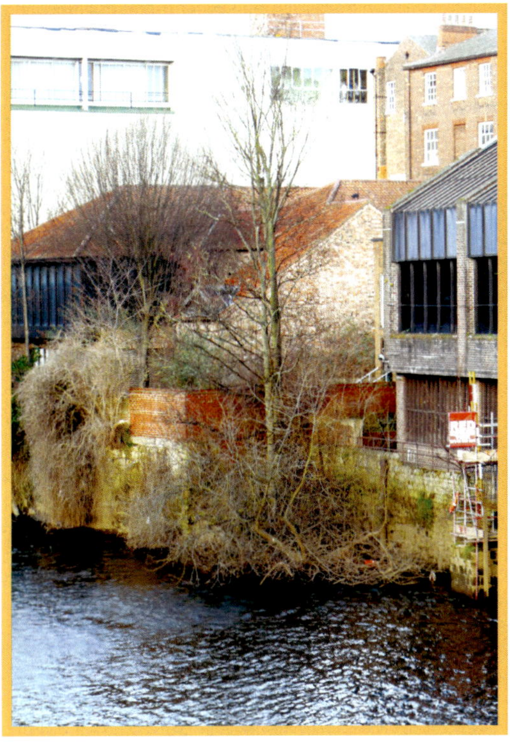

Cat K: The Peering Cat of Coney Street
Location: Coney Street

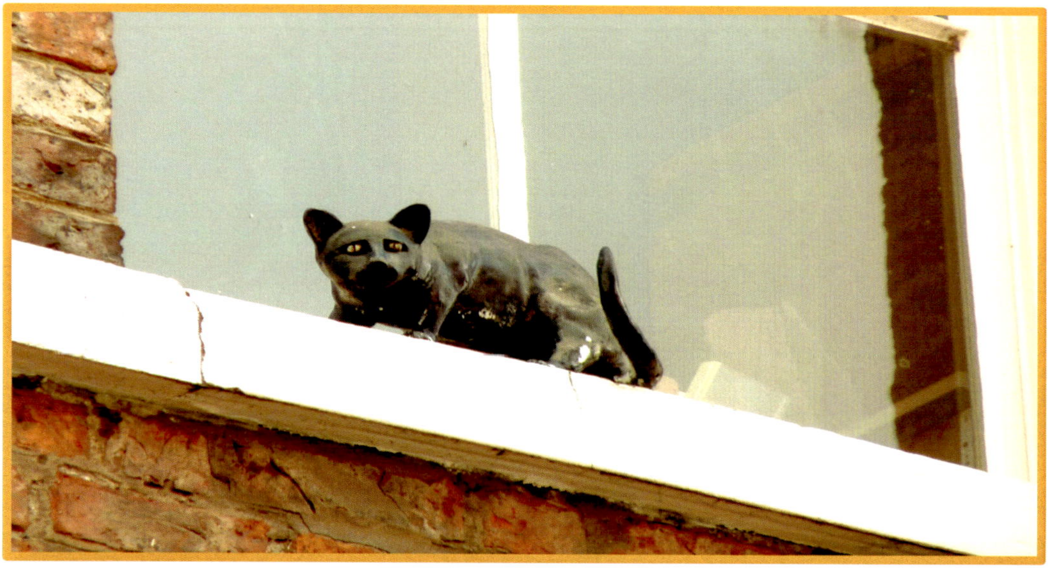

This cat, peering over Coney Street, is one of the earliest placed by Tom Adams as a signature of his work. It featured in an article in the York Evening Press in January 1982 and has a partner on the other side of the building overlooking the river. See the previous page.

The Sculptor is Jonathan Newdick and the cat is made of black resin, with luminous eyes.

At the time of going to print the shop below the cat is empty. It was a branch of 'Mothercare' when the cat was installed and, latterly, 'Clinton Cards'.

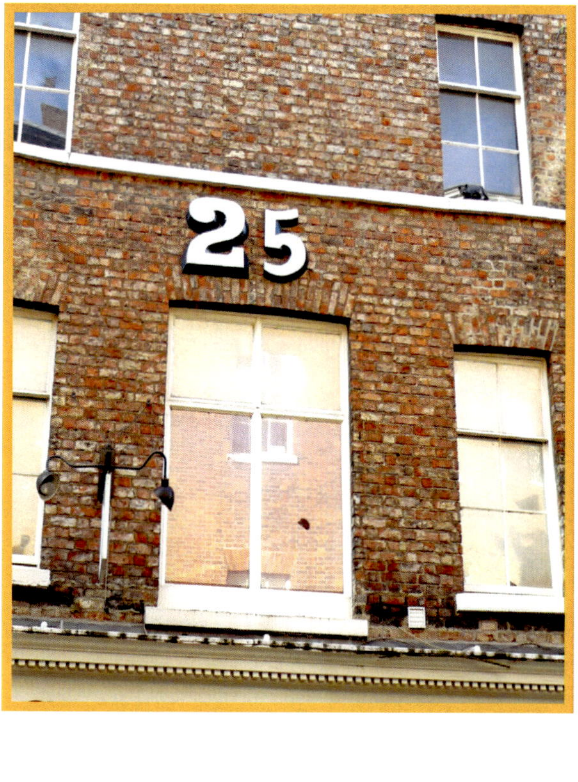

Cat L: Chambers...the cat
Location: Museum Street

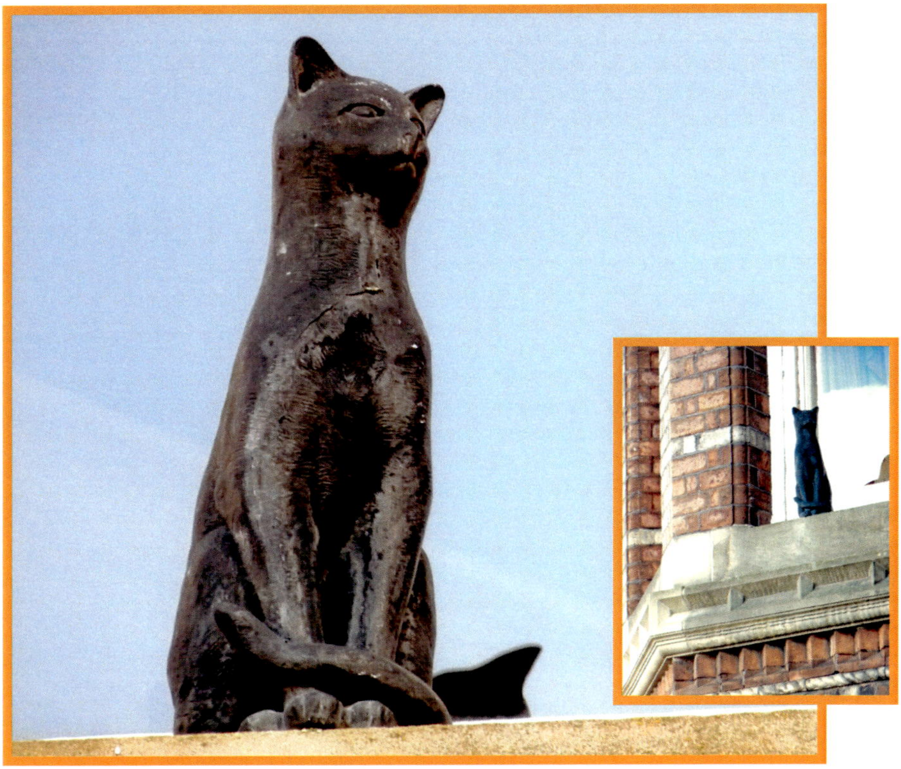

This handsome cat has been called Chambers ever since his owners had him installed on the first floor of their building called: Chambers! His personal history appears to have been lost as no one seems to know much about him but he is holding his own up there! He is tough and resilient, being made of resin. Note the rather superior pose, upright and proud, with tail neatly curled across his paws.
He is watching over the busy road below and facing across to the Museum gardens.
He is, of course, a Jonathan Newdick cat.

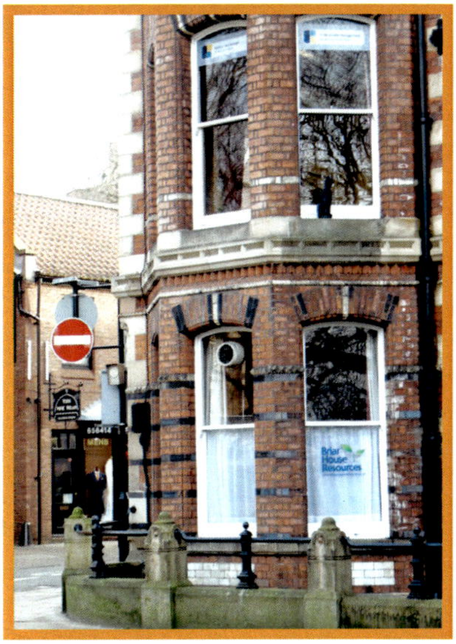

Cat M: The Architects Cat…still at the office
Location: 105 The Mount

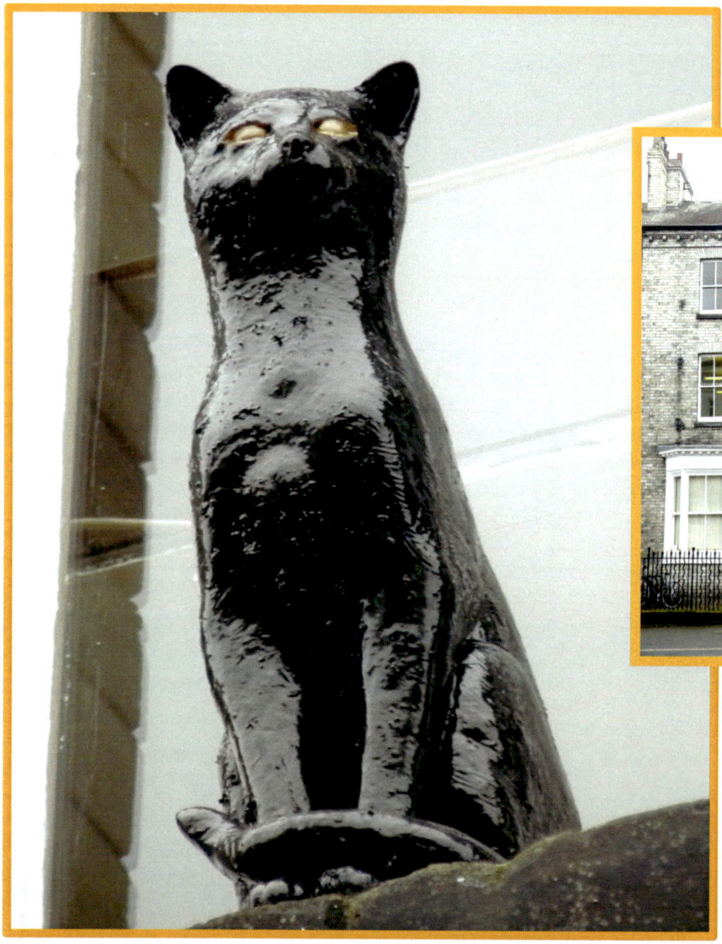

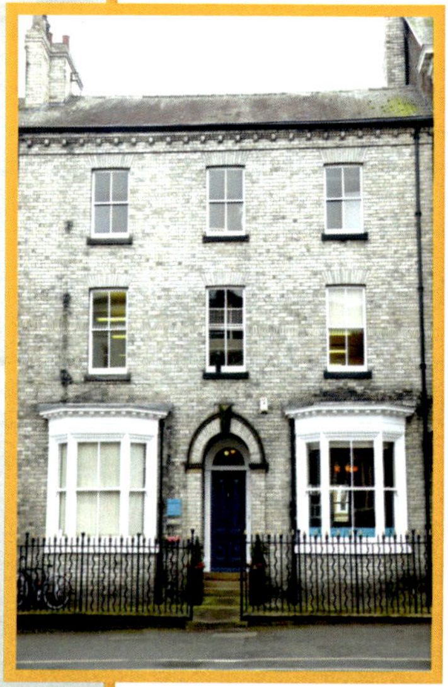

This is a very important cat as he sits on the windowsill above the front door of the house that was Tom Adams' office. He was 'The Boss's cat'! He is still there today acting as a landmark for the current owners' business.

He has been painted recently so is looking loved and well-cared for, unlike some of Yorks other cats! Like some others he has luminous eyes. Notice how neatly his tail is curled over his front paws. Apparently a contented cat at peace with his situation! We think Tom Adams would be pleased.
He was made by Jonathan Newdick and installed in 1982. Photographs of that period show it surrounded by Virginia Creeper but sadly that has gone, leaving this cat looking rather exposed and isolated and the building bare.

Cat N: The Cat and the Lamp
Location: Gillygate

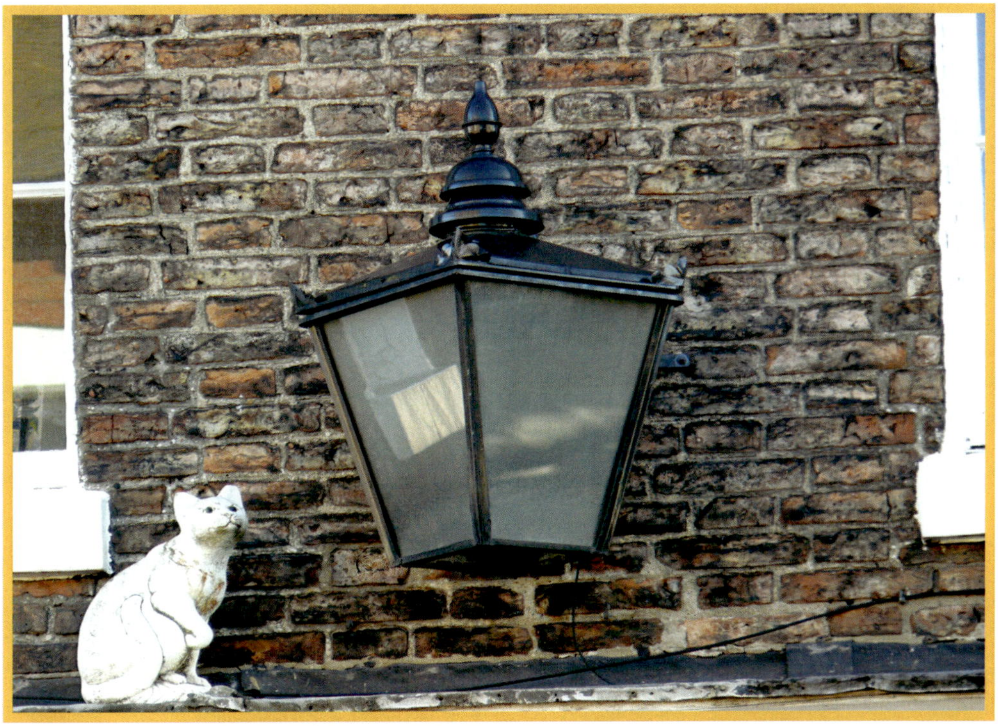

You will recognise this lonely but appealing little cat if you travel along Gillygate, especially if you are on the upper floor of the bus.

This white cat is made of concrete and we are told it was bought from a garden centre (so, not a Tom Adams cat!) and put in place during the 1980's by the person who lived in the flat above the shop.
At some point the cat was stolen but, thankfully, the thief dumped it beside a lamppost nearby. It was swiftly returned to its original position, so at least one of it's lives has been used up!

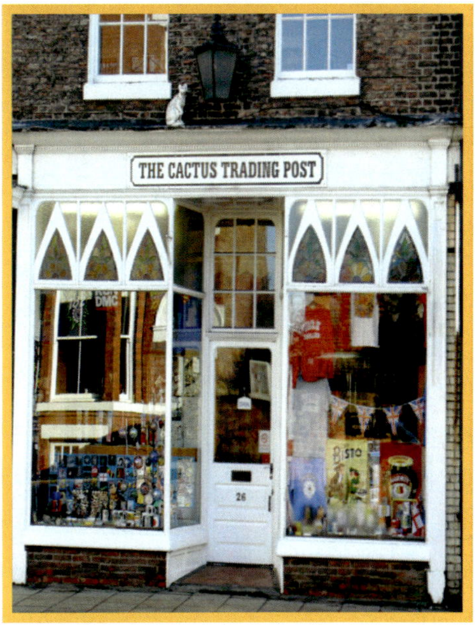

Cat O: The Sad One Eyed Cat

Location: Stonegate

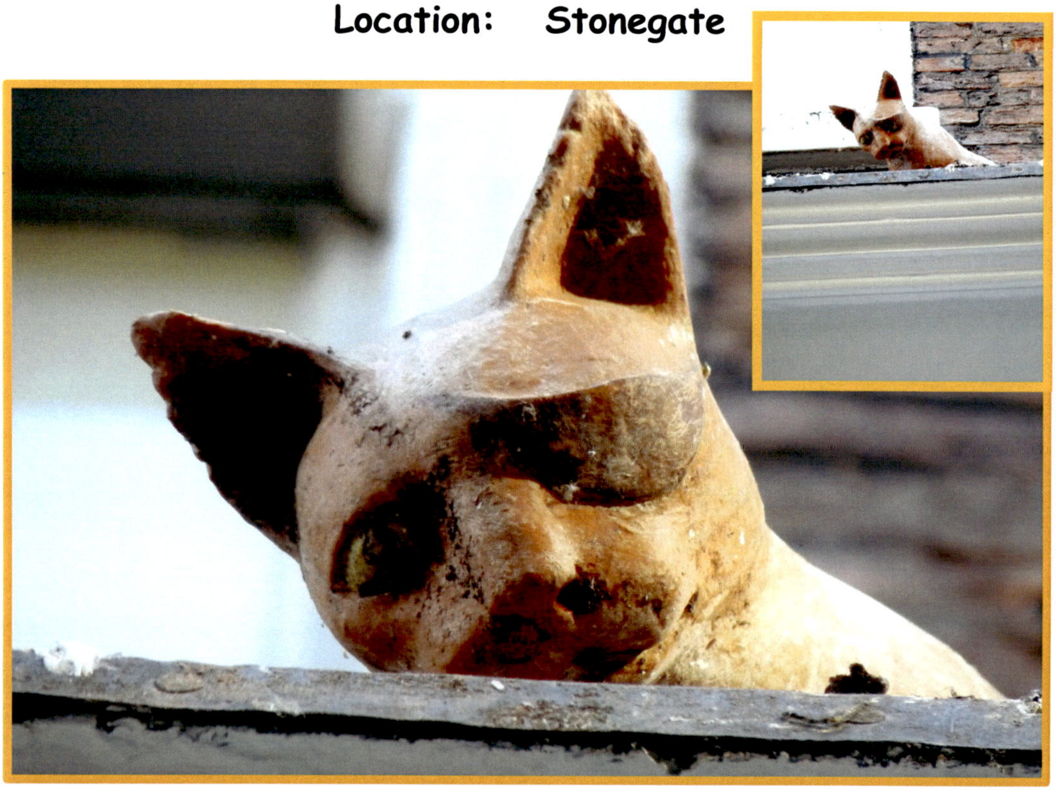

We are told that this is 'Gordon', the one eyed cat who peers over the doorway at No. 35a Stonegate, all on his own, no other cats nearby!

Very little appears to be known about poor Gordon's origins. It has been reported that he was modelled on a real cat who was born without eyelids on one eye and wore an eyepatch to prevent infections. His peering pose from his ledge makes him look as though he would love some attention. Further research is needed to find out more about this unusual and rather sad member of the York cats' trail.

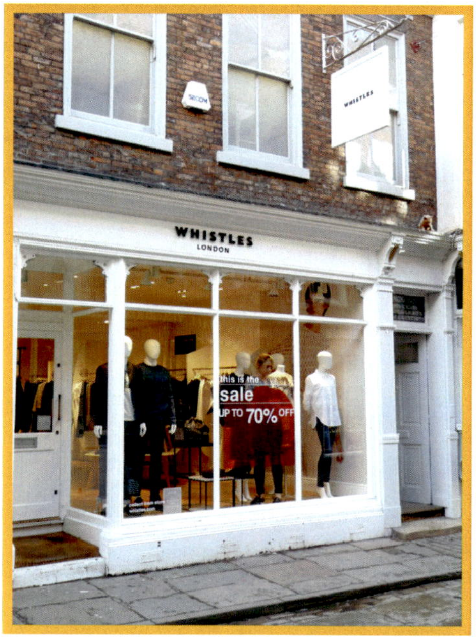

Cat P: The Gallery Cat
Location: Low Petergate

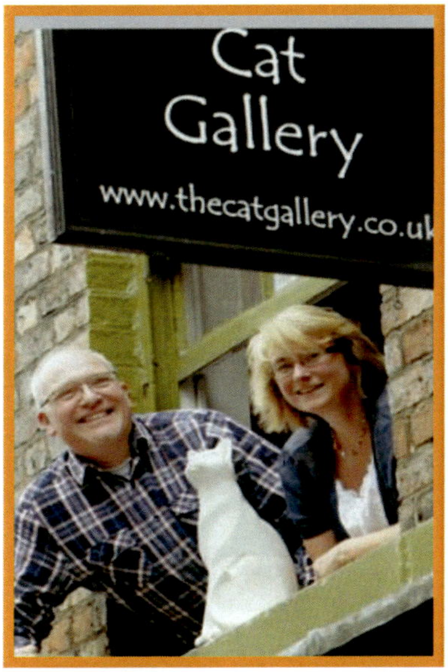

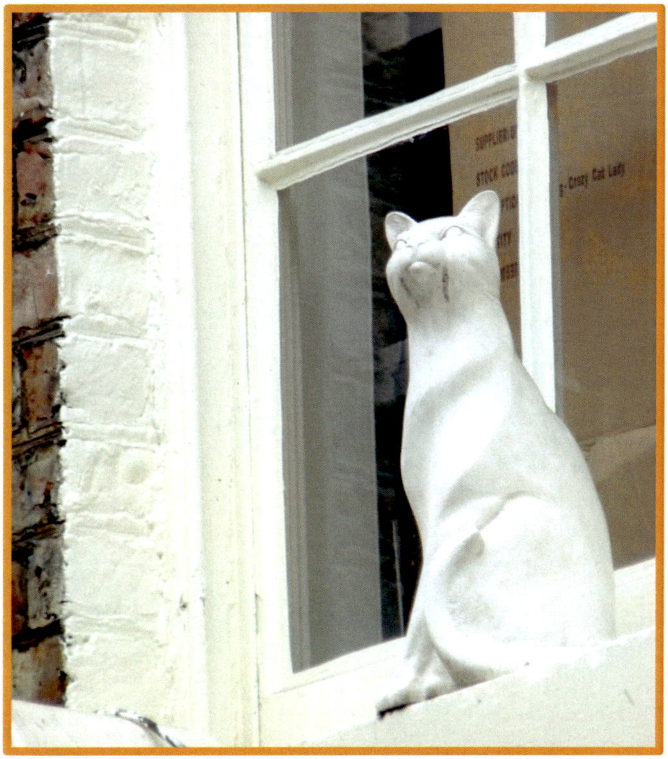

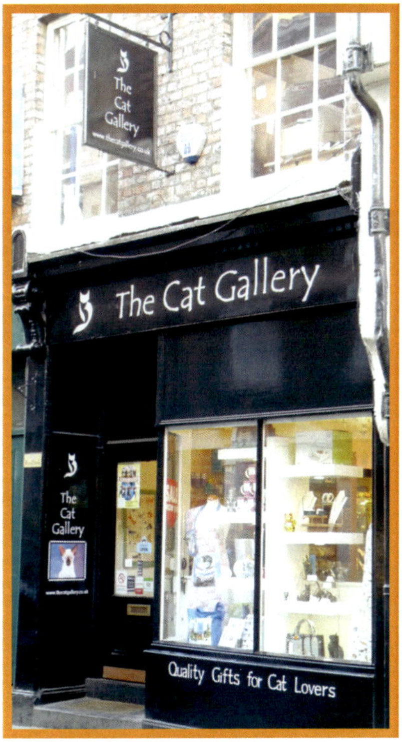

It seems entirely appropriate that the 'Cat Gallery' in Low Petergate has it's own cat! This one strikes a proud and dignified pose, complete with flowing body curves and a neatly curled tail.
When the owners moved into the shop in 2010 to sell all manner of cat related gifts they had to ensure that they were on the 'cat trail' of York so they commissioned this model and developed a leaflet and map to accompany the 'cat trail'.

The Gallery Cat is shown above with Jonathan Newdick and Alison Hanson before being secured in place. It featured in the York Press in July 2011.

Cat Q: The New Comer of the 21st. Century
Location: The Shambles

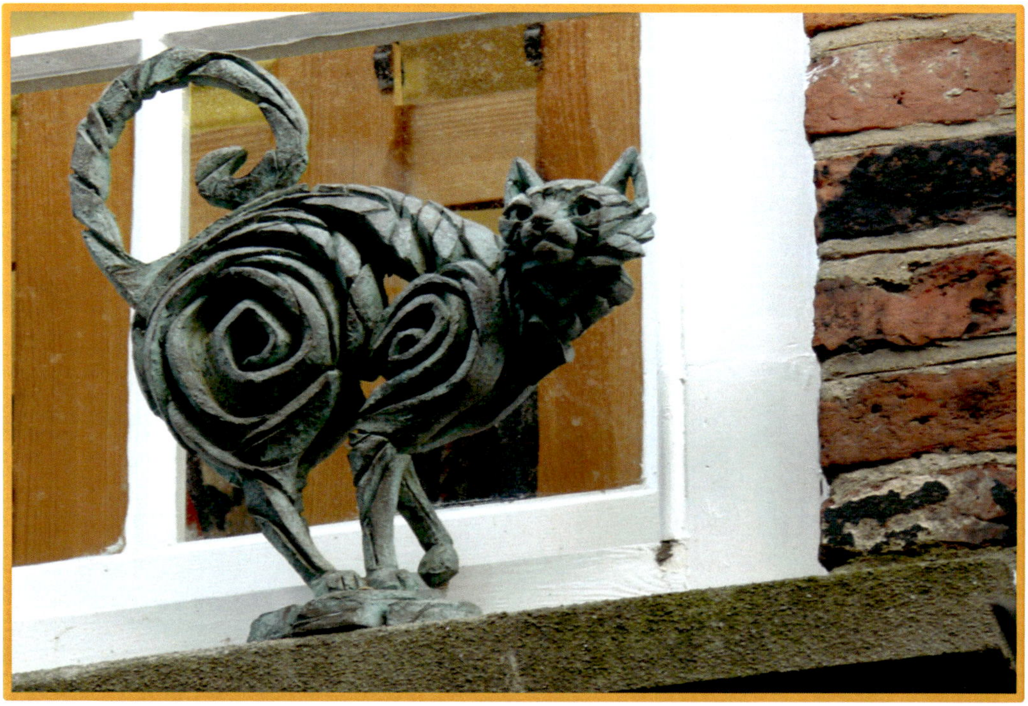

This newcomer illustrates that the tradition of cats being placed on York buildings continues!

The Manager of the Edinburgh Woollen Mill shop, just opposite York Glass (see next page), in The Shambles arranged for this very modern, rather forbidding, cat to be placed on the windowsill above the shop front recently. It was purchased commercially so the origins are not known.

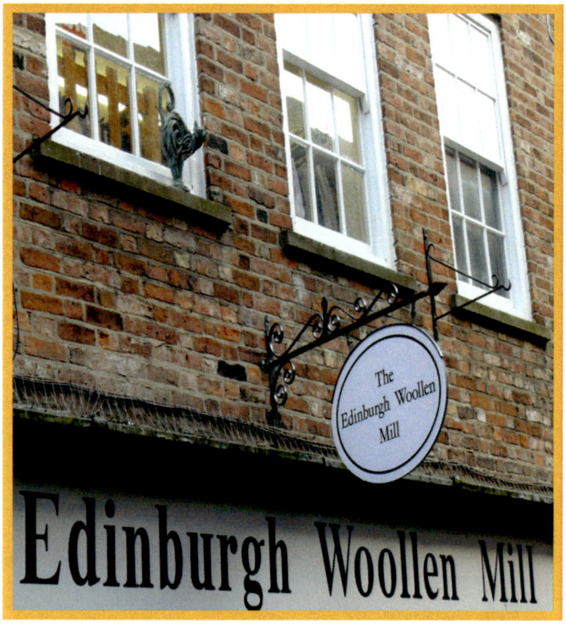

Cat R: The Clinging Cat
Location: The Shambles

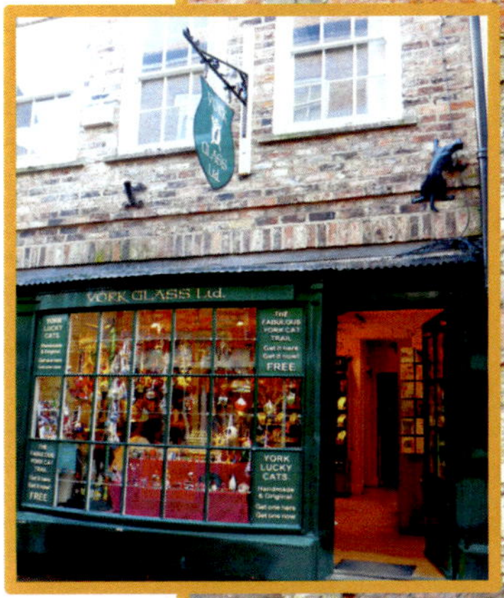

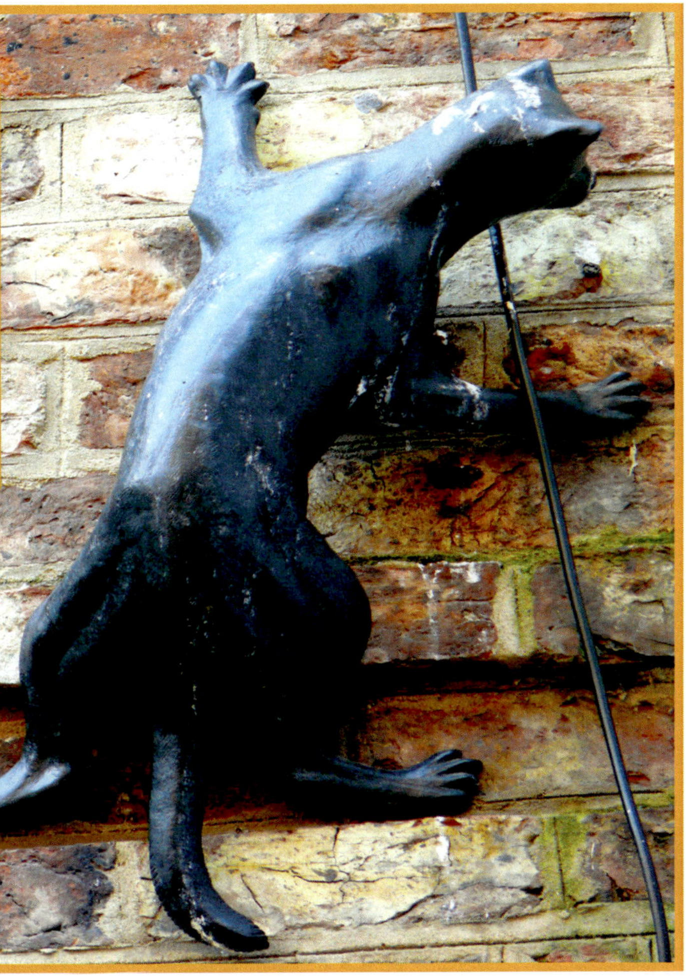

York Glass is the home of one of the Cat Trails where leaflets including a map can be obtained. This cat was made by Jonathan Newdick at the request of the shop owner in The Shambles and was installed in 2011. It is modelled on Tom Adam's own cat 'Mickey' who liked to climb the walls of Tom's office (see page 25).
It is clinging to the wall just opposite the 'new arrival' on the Edinburgh Woollen Mill shop opposite (see previous page). Perhaps it doesn't like its territory being invaded or, we think, it might be climbing the wall to scare off the pigeons that roost on the windowsills next to the doorway of the Margaret Clitheroe shrine.

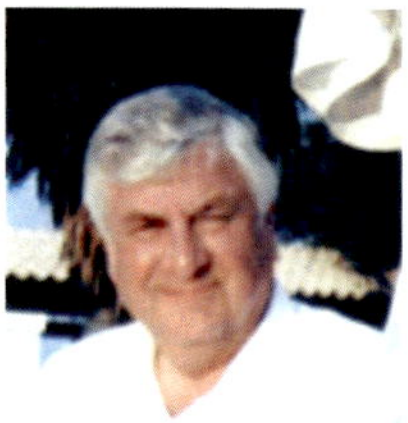

The Architect....Tom Adams

Tom Adams was one of Yorks' best-known architects. He was born in Halifax in 1930 and went on to train at the Birmingham School of Architecture in the 1950's. There he met Geoffrey Darke, who later formed the London firm Dearborn and Darke. One day Geoffrey said "Why don't you sign your sketches with a cat, because Leonardo da Vinci signed his with a mouse and your cat will eat the mouse!" From then on, most of Tom's sketches were adorned with a cat, somewhere on the parchment and he continued his love of cats, often purchasing special Cat Art or by owning his own cat.

During the war, Tom was posted to the Northern Command Office in York and vividly recalled stepping out of the train station to the sight of the city walls covered in daffodils. He immediately fell in love with the city.

After a short time in Leeds, he secured his first post-war job with the York City Architects department under Ernie Hurst and then with Bradleys and Shepherds of York. This lead on to fellowship of the Royal Institute of British Architects, his own design consultancy and a long and distinguished career designing over 1500 projects in and around York as well as in London, Scotland and Ireland.

Tom was a familiar and eccentric figure in the business life of York. He worked on a wide range of commercial and domestic buildings. His best known architectural works include the champagne bar at York Racecourse, the Royal York Hotel, Woods Mill, Skeldergate, Foss Islands House, The RSPCA Home, and the Catholic Chaplaincy at the University of York.

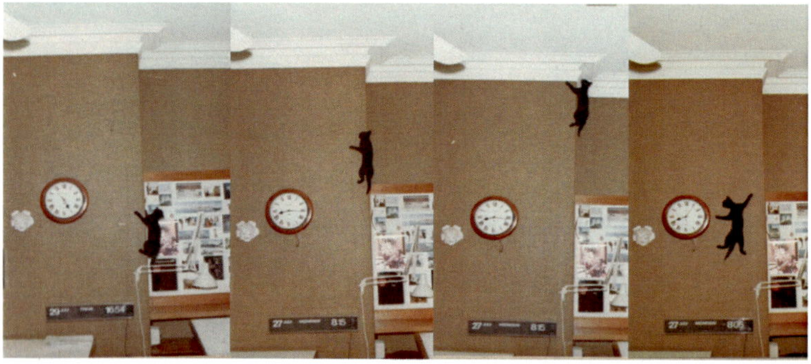

Photos of Tom's cat "Mickey" climbing the hessian wallpaper at his architectural practice at 105 The Mount, which also boasts a cat sculpture on its façade.

It was in 1979 that he placed the first black cat sculpture at 25 Coney Street when the building was occupied by Mothercare and, more recently by Clinton Cards. He placed cats on those buildings, which he had, either, designed or had worked on in some other way, e.g. restoration, renovation or repair, as a kind of signature. Tom saw this as a way of contributing to what he described as the 'magic fabric' of York. He once said, "There should be fun in Architecture and that is why the cats are here". The fact that so many of the cats still reside where he put them, with more being added, and the development of the 'cat trails' by two galleries is testament to Tom's idea being shared by many, many people. The magazine 'Cat World' even featured his work in a picture spread. The collage of press cuttings below gives some idea of how much coverage was given to his work in York.

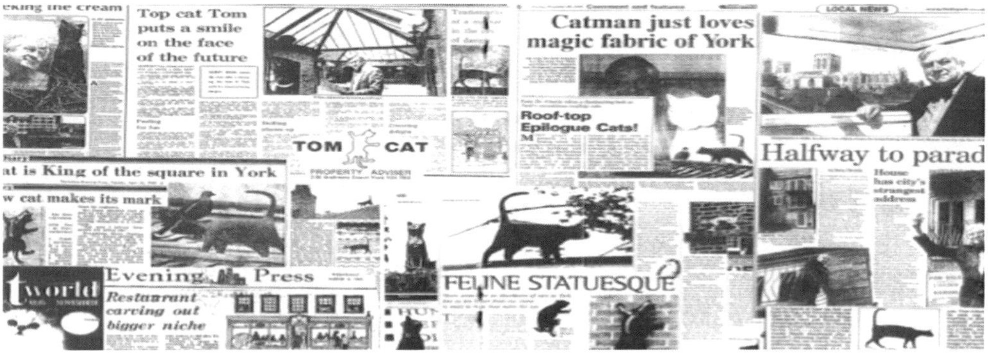

Tom commissioned York Sculptor Jonathan Newdick to make the cats and they worked closely together for many years.

On Wednesday 1st February 2006 The York Press newspaper announced Tom's death, aged 75. One of Tom's long standing friends said; "Tom was one of those people whose company you always wished you didn't have to leave. Tom was a true man of York and just loved it. His fun, gossip, jokes and limitless supply of ideas, coupled with his professionalism, made him unique".

The Sculptor.........Jonathan Newdick MRBS

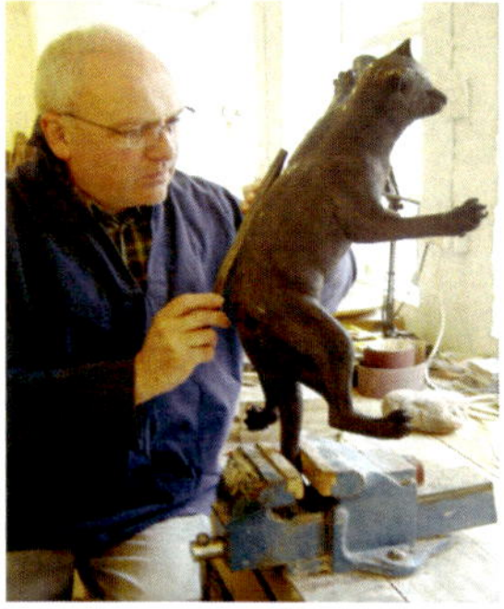

Jonathan has been making sculptures for over 30 years and was elected a member of the Royal British Society of Sculptors in 2004.

In addition to teaching, Jonathan works from his studio in York carving sculptures in wood, stone and bronze. After being commissioned by Tom Adams, Jonathan visited the RSPCA refuge in York and drew some sketches on which he based the first cat statues. "I would tap on the glass of their cages and the cats would come up to the glass inquisitively, so I could draw them in my sketchbook". It was sad to think they were not long for this world, but they were the inspiration for cat sculptures that would be part of York's architecture for many years to come"

Later, Jonathan was inspired by Tom's own cat called "Mickey" as a model for one of the sculptures. Jonathan has made cat sculptures for 14 of York's buildings within the city walls to date, 10 on the outskirts of York, and others have found homes in Cardiff, Washington USA, and Madras in India.

The cats are designed and modelled in clay then a mould is made, from which the cat sculpture is cast, using glass reinforced polyester resin. Each cat sculpture can take 3 to 6 weeks to make. Jonathan is responsible for each process from design, through to the finished feline. When the cat sculpture is finished it is then carefully positioned on the building, and securely fixed; to the roof, window sill, wall or even a narrow railing, as required by the client.

The photograph above shows Jonathan working on the cat now adorning Barnitts, in Kings Square. Jonathan is still making cat sculptures today, and he will be placing a few more on buildings in York...look out for them!

You can also see some of his cats and figurative sculptures at the Pyramid Gallery, 43 Stonegate, York.

Also, visit his website at www.newdicksculpture.co.uk if you are interested in contacting Jonathan.
His e mail address is :
j_newdick@hotmail.co.uk.

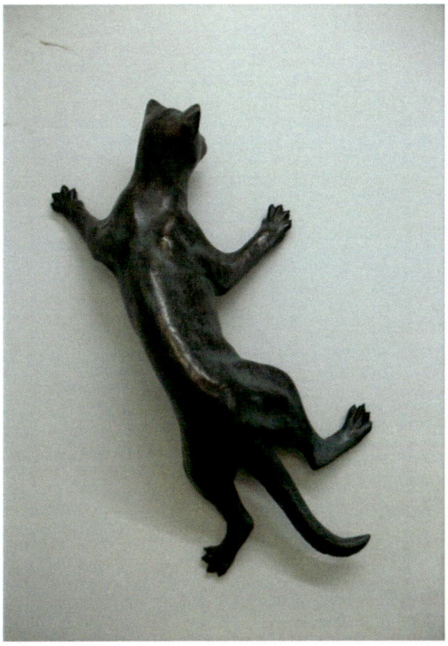

Climbing cat sculpture based on Mickey, the cat who used to like climbing up the hessian wallpaper of Tom Adam's office. (See Page 25)

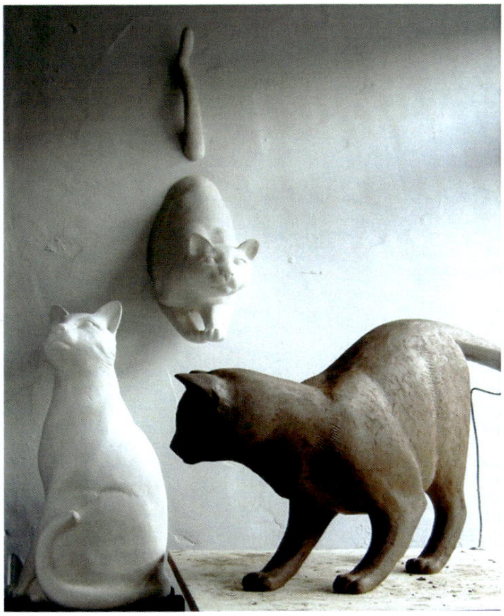

Life in the Studio

It is rare for three of these cats to ever be seen together since they are destined to live rather singular lives on their respective 'sites'!

This unique shot shows:

- the 'Ghost cat' which lives at the front of a spooky building in York, 'The Golden Fleece' Pub in Pavement, York. (See page 13)
- the superior looking white cat sits on the Cat Gallery windowsill in Low Petergate. (See page 22) and,
- the brown cat, still in the clay stage in this photo, now lives in Cardiff.

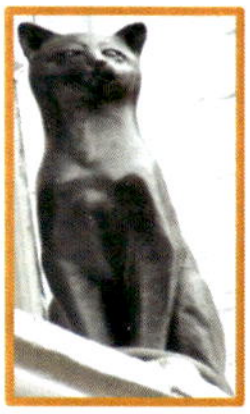

Some random Facts and Fictions about Black Cats………… (no responsibility can be accepted for accuracy or otherwise!)

- Many famous people have written about their cats and the important part their pet played in their lives. Among them are: Emily Bronte, Patrick Moore, Ernst Hemingway, Christina Rossetti, Mark Twain, Edward Lear, Raymond Chandler and Thomas Huxley. Even 10 Downing Street had a famous cat.

- The Scots believe that a strange black cats' arrival to the home signifies prosperity. In Japan black cats are considered to bring good luck. In Germany some believe that black cats crossing a person's path from the right to left is a bad omen whereas if it crosses from left to right the cat is granting favourable times.

- The idea that black cats were viewed favourably seems to come from the Egyptian Goddess 'Bast' (or 'Bastet'), the cat Goddess. Egyptian households believed they could gain favour from this Goddess if they had a black cat in their household. Even Charles 1st is said to have felt that all his luck disappeared after the death of his treasured black cat. Sailors would often have a black cat as they considered it brought good luck. Sailors wives would often have black cats too in the hope their their influence would help to protect their husbands whilst at sea.

- In Western Society, we are told that black cats have often been thought of as an evil omen, in league with witches! Pilgrims arriving at Plymouth Rock apparently banned anyone from having a black cat. The gambling world is afraid of black cats, believing if, while travelling to a casino, a black cat crosses a gambler's road or path, that the person should not go to the casino as the cat will bring bad luck.

- It was thought that black cat statues would frighten away rats and mice which might have carried plague and illness.

- I have even read that a lady who owns a black cat will have many suitors. I have not even attempted to verify the truth or otherwise of this claim!